come into the mountains, dear friend

Other books by

𝕭lue 𝕸ountain 𝕬rts inc.

I Want to Laugh, I Want to Cry
by Susan Polis Schutz
Peace Flows from the Sky
by Susan Pols Schutz

The Best Is Yet to Be
The International Grandmothers' Cookbook
Step to the Music You Hear, Vol. I
Step to the Music You Hear, Vol. II
The Desiderata of Happiness
The Language of Friendship
Whatever Is, Is Best
Poor Richard's Quotations
The Language of Love

come into the mountains, dear friend

a collection of poems
By
susan polis schutz

designed and illustrated by
stephen schutz

Blue
Mountain
Arts inc.
Boulder, Colorado

library of congress catalog card number 72-88699
international standard book number 0-88396-001-X

manufactured in the united states of america

blue mountain arts, inc.
p. o. box 4549
boulder, colorado 80303

First Printing   October, 1972
Second Printing   January, 1973
Third Printing   August, 1973
Fourth Printing   November, 1973
Fifth Printing   January, 1974
Sixth Printing   December, 1974
Seventh Printing November, 1975

contents

introduction

the world turns around, new people grow up, and still the inhuman forces that society imposes against the individual are present. I believe that we can eliminate these evils through love and friendship.

come into the mountains, dear friend, to seek out the beautiful things in the world so that you can use these positive forces to create a new and better world.

s.p.s.

thoughts

come into the mountains, dear friend
leave society and take no one with you
but your true self
get close to nature
your everyday games will be insignificant
notice the clouds spontaneously forming patterns
and try to do that with your life

a man is only complete
when he has a true friend
to understand him,
to share all his
passions and sorrows with,
and to stand by him
throughout his life.

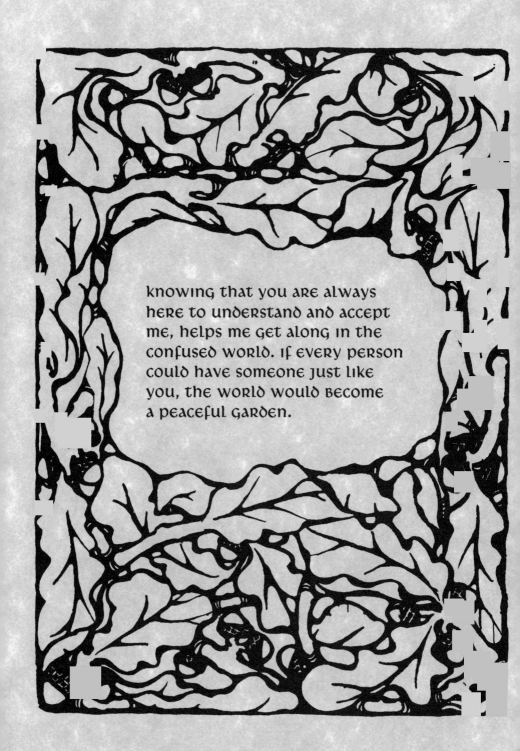

knowing that you are always
here to understand and accept
me, helps me get along in the
confused world. if every person
could have someone just like
you, the world would become
a peaceful garden.

our friendship has taken on new meaning
in the long time since
we traded comic books and shared the same heroes.

now we rarely see each other,
but when we do meet,
we sit for hours discussing our lives
and it is as though we never parted.

it is comforting to know
that whatever happens, whether good or bad,
there is a friend who will understand.

you know how i feel
you listen to how i think
you understand...
            you're
            my
            friend

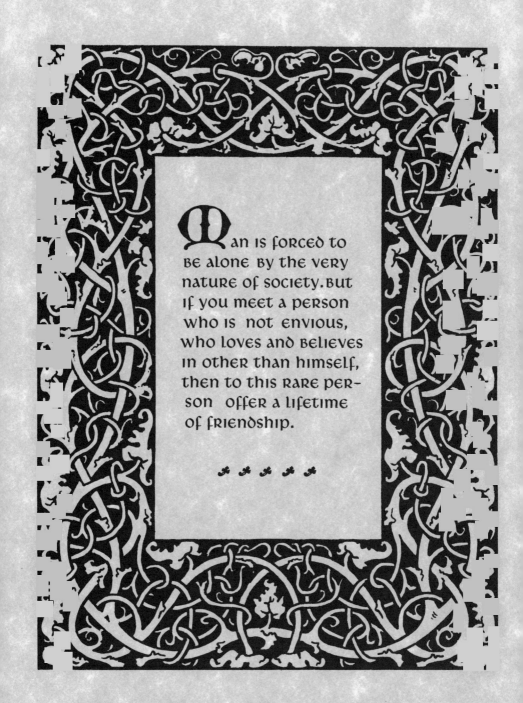

ℳan is forced to be alone by the very nature of society. But if you meet a person who is not envious, who loves and believes in other than himself, then to this rare person offer a lifetime of friendship.

❧ ❧ ❧ ❧

many a sun set
since i last saw you
when we played
in our tree hut
and planned our lives,
you, a teacher-to-be,
me, a writer-to-be.

now, fifteen autumns later,
we meet.
you, smelling of lemon cosmetics, dressed
                            in the latest fashion,
me, with my faded jeans and turtleneck.
you, with three little children that look
                            just like you,
me, with my three unpublished manuscripts.
you, with your shiny dishwasher and
                            wall to wall carpeting,
me, with my paper plates. . . .

but you living your life through others
and me living my own life with others.

we parted with tears,
each looking at the other with pity.
knowing that we had very little left in common,
we both wished that perhaps there were
enough to keep our friendship alive,
even if just to meet each other occasionally to see
how another segment of the world lives.

"can you type?"
"no!"
"can you file?"
"no!"
"can you take shorthand?"
"no!"
"how about simple bookkeeping?"
"no!"
"what on earth can you do?"
"everything you can!"

we are women-people
free to do what we want
live the way we choose
look the way we like
say the way we feel

you must all accept this

beautiful green and yellow weed,
they say to cut you down quickly
before you spread throughout the neighborhood.

you look just like a flower to me,
only a little stronger.
don't feel bad because they call you
a health hazard.
feel sad that they are so prejudiced.
you know they are like that with people too.

i will never cut you down.
i want a garden of weeds.
please spread your seedlings densely
and thank you for making the ground enchanted.

we need to feel more
to understand others.
we need to love more
to be loved back.
we need to cry more
to cleanse ourselves.
we need to laugh more
to enjoy ourselves.
we need to see more
other than our own little fantasies.
we need to hear more
and listen to the needs of others.
we need to give more
and take less.
we need to share more
and own less.
we need to look more
and realize that we are not so different
                         from one another.
we need to create a world where
all can peacefully live the life they choose.

feelings

in the morning
when the sun
is just starting to light the day,
i am awakened
and my first thoughts are of you.

at night
i stare at the dark trees
silhouetted against the quiet stars,
i am entranced into a complete peacefulness
and my last thoughts are of you.

your heart is my heart
    your truth is my truth
        your feeling is my feeling

but the real strength of our love
is that we share rather than
control each other's lives

how beautiful it is
when acting and being are one
no crying when laughing
no sadness when happiness

my emotions have been softened
my body possessed
i am independent
but captured

with you there
and me here
i have had no one
to discuss little things with
like how the dew feels on the grass
or big things like
what's going on in the world

i have been lonely
talking and thinking to myself
i now realize how essential it is
to have someone
to share oneself with

the sand looks out on the rippling water
the sky has cast an omnipotent dimness
each wave crashes against the shore
washing the shells to mingle with the pebbles

we are so tiny
staring at the ocean
i wonder what other than
nature is significant

in the quiet hours
we listen to the human songs of
joan baez
and we are
one emotion
together
in
a
tear

our souls touch
our hearts feel
our bodies meet
and we are
one
complete
allness

what is life to you?
the butterflies among the tulips
the children rolling down the grassy hills
the sun feeding the seeds of fertility
finding someone whose sensitive expression
makes you cry . . .

our special spot
where the clear sky forms a roof
over the greens and browns;
nature's unplanned blending.

the peaceful singing of the birds
makes us forget the world outside
and i only want to live in this environment
with our love as pure and beautiful
as nature surrounding us.

everywhere rose mountains of sand
making us very tiny
the night wind drew us together
and the crackling fire warmed our feet
we were in the sky
or we were on a desert in the biblical days
and you were moses climbing the mountain
surrounded by peaceful barrenness and love

it is so nice being with you
somehow the grass feels softer
and the birds seem to sing just for us

the world is warmer
when one has someone to hide with

sometimes i wake up ecstatic
realizing that i am me
different from everyone else
yet the same
i look me
i think me
i feel me
but me alone is not complete
so i have joined you

air so fresh and clear
the silence echoes the chirping of the crickets
we're holding hands
watching not to step on the ants today

our hearts are open
because right now, everything appears so peaceful
it's a beautiful day
and it has temporarily overwhelmed us

when i am working
you are with me
when i am playing
you are with me
when i am alone
you are with me

even though we may be apart
you are always
with me

surrounded by the
fragrance of blossoming grass
I am alive with a love
of life and a feeling
of oneness with
the earth

let us dance in the sun
wearing wild flowers in our hair
and let us huddle together
as darkness takes over

we are at home amidst the
                birds and the trees
        for we are
        children of nature

ABOUT THE AUTHORS

Susan and Stephen Schutz presently live in Boulder, Colorado. Their poetry and illustrations have appeared on over a million notecards and prints, and have drawn exceptional response from numerous readers.

After attending graduate school, Susan worked as a teacher, a social worker, a public relations writer, and a newspaper reporter. Then she pursued her career in freelance writing. She has had many articles published in magazines and newspapers and has written several volumes of poetry. She is currently working on an autobiographical novel.

Stephen studied at the New York High School of Music and Art, the Boston Museum of Fine Arts School, the Massachusetts Institute of Technology, and received a Ph.D. from Princeton University in 1970. He is known for his original calligraphy and serigraph techniques, and has won awards for design.